FIRST PEOPLES
THE CREE
OF NORTH AMERICA

DEBORAH B. ROBINSON

Lerner Publications Company • Minneapolis

**First American edition published in 2002
by Lerner Publications Company**

Published by arrangement with Times Editions
Copyright © 2002 by Times Media Private Limited

Lerner Publications Company
A division of Lerner Publishing Group
241 First Avenue North
Minneapolis, MN 55401 U.S.A.
Website address: www.lernerbooks.com

Series originated and designed by
Times Editions
An imprint of Times Media Private Limited
A member of the Times Publishing Group
1 New Industrial Road, Singapore 536196
Website address: www.timesone.com.sg/te

Series editors: Margaret J. Goldstein, Scott Marsh
Series designers: Tuck Loong, Jailani Basari
Series picture researcher: Susan Jane Manuel

Library of Congress Cataloging-in-Publication Data
Robinson, Deborah B.
The Cree of North America / by Deborah B. Robinson.— 1st American ed.
p. cm. — (First peoples)
Includes bibliographical references and index.
Summary: Describes the history, modern and traditional cultural practices and economies,
geographic background, and ongoing oppression and struggles of the Cree.
ISBN 0-8225-4178-5 (lib. bdg. : alk. paper)
1. Cree Indians—Juvenile literature. [1. Cree Indians. 2. Indians of North America—Canada.]
I. Title. II. Series.
E99.C88 R63 2002
971.2004'973—dc21   2001004236

Printed in Malaysia
Bound in the United States of America

1 2 3 4 5 6—OS—07 06 05 04 03 02

CONTENTS

WHO ARE THE CREE?

The Cree are a large group of Native American people. Most Cree live in Canada, although some live in the United States. The Cree live in different bands, or small groups, which are named after the places they live. These bands include the Eastern Cree, Plains Cree, Woodlands Cree, East and West Swampy Cree, Moose Cree, and Attikamek Cree. Cree people live throughout most of Canada, from Newfoundland in the east to Alberta in the west. In the United States, most Cree live in Montana. In all, about 200,000 Cree live in Canada, and about 8,000 Cree live in the United States. Traditionally, the Cree spoke a form of Algonquian, a Native American language. Most also speak English or French, the main languages spoken in Canada.

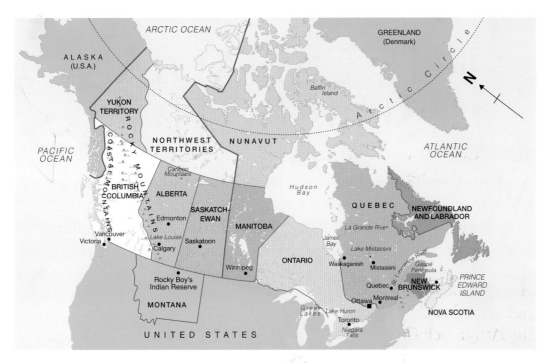

Many Names

Native Americans are sometimes called Indians. In Canada, Native American groups are also called First Nations, because they were the first people to live there. Originally, Cree who lived in different places had different names for themselves. The Cree got their modern name from French fur traders, who called them Kristineaux. Later, this name was shortened to Kri, spelled Cree in English.

A Changing Lifestyle

For thousands of years, the Cree hunted, fished, and gathered wild plants for food. They traveled from place to place in search of fresh food supplies. When Europeans arrived in Canada in the 1600s, many Cree began to trade beaver and other animal furs with the newcomers. Gradually, the Cree began to settle around fur trading posts. Most modern Cree hold ordinary jobs. Some live in big cities. But they also try to preserve their ancient traditions.

A MIXED HERITAGE

When French explorers and traders first came to Canada in the 1600s, many of them married native women, especially Cree women. Their children were called Métis, which means "mixed" in French. The name Métis is still used to describe Canadians of mixed native and white heritage.

THE CANADIAN SUBARCTIC

Most Cree live in the subarctic region of Canada. This is an area south of the Arctic Circle. The Arctic Circle is an imaginary line around the Earth, 1,624 miles (2,613 kilometers) south of the North Pole. North of the Arctic Circle is a place called the Arctic, the northernmost region on Earth.

Below: Small plants and shrubs grow in the Canadian tundra.

The Tree Line

The Arctic Circle is not an actual line on the ground. It is an imaginary line, found only on maps. What really separates the Arctic and subarctic zones is a boundary called the tree line. Above this boundary, trees cannot grow because the weather is too cold. Only shrubs, grasses, and other small plants can survive there. Forests of spruce, pine, and larch trees grow south of the tree line. These forests are called taiga. The treeless region above the tree line is called the tundra.

Above: The warmer weather south of the tree line allows forests to thrive.

Frozen Soil

Subarctic lands are very cold. In some places, the soil is frozen almost all year long. This frozen soil is called permafrost. It contains a lot of ice. When the land becomes warmer during the summer, the ice in the top layer of soil thaws. But the ice below remains frozen. This frozen layer keeps the water in the top layer from flowing down into the ground. The soil becomes very soggy. The water trapped at the top forms ponds and bogs that provide moisture for plants.

THE CANADIAN SHIELD

The Canadian Shield is a huge mass of rock lying beneath most of Cree country. It covers almost 1,900,000 square miles (4,900,000 square kilometers). Scientists think the shield formed more than 3.8 billion years ago. It is thought to contain some of the oldest rocks on earth. The shield has hills, ridges, valleys, and boggy areas. It also contains rivers and shallow lakes (*below*).

A LAND OF SNOW AND ICE

I n the center of Canada, large masses of cold air hang over the land in winter, creating very cold weather. Winters are long and very cold in most of Cree territory. There is lots of snow. Even in summer, Cree lands do not get very warm.

Freezing Temperatures

During winter in the Canadian subarctic, temperatures below 0 degrees Fahrenheit (-17.8 degrees Celsius) are common. Sometimes temperatures are lower than -50 degrees Fahrenheit (-45.6 degrees Celsius). Summers are short and cool. High temperatures average just 48 to 68 degrees Fahrenheit (9 to 20 degrees Celsius) in the Canadian subarctic in summer.

Below: Traveling by boat becomes difficult for the Cree once lakes start to freeze.

Above: These spruce trees in Quebec are covered by the first snows of winter.

Heavy Snowfalls

Many places in Cree territory get more then 30 inches (76 centimeters) of snow each year. The depth of the snow varies from place to place. Often, the wind blows snow from high or open areas into valleys or against hillsides. This creates tall banks of snow called snowdrifts. Snow that falls in winter melts in spring and flows into lakes and rivers.

GLOBAL WARMING

Temperatures on Earth have increased in the last one hundred years. This increase is called global warming. If global warming continues, it could bring big changes to the subarctic. For example, higher temperatures would melt permafrost. Melted areas would become boggy. Melting ice (*below*) could also flood the land. Warmer temperatures in summer would bring more insects to the subarctic. Some of these insects might carry disease. Many scientists think that air pollution has caused global warming. People are working to reduce air pollution to keep temperatures from increasing further.

A LAND OF EVERGREEN FORESTS

Plants of the subarctic region must be able to survive the long, cold winters. Plants found north of the tree line include mosses, lichens, shrubs, and miniature trees. They take root in the thin layer of soil that thaws in summer. Below the tree line, forests are filled with conifer trees, or evergreens. Poplar and white birch trees often grow among the evergreens.

Below: Conifer trees grow in many forests below the tree line.

Surviving in Cold Weather

The most common trees in the Canadian subarctic are conifers. Examples of conifers include spruce and pine trees. Their leaves grow all year-round, which is why conifers are also called evergreens. Most conifers have needle-shaped leaves.

Left: Conifers have tough leaves that can withstand cold temperatures.

Bogs in the Forest

Canadian subarctic forests contain bogs. Bogs are shallow lakes that fill up with decayed plants. The decayed plants often form a thick mat that floats on the water. Small shrubs, flowers, and other plants often grow on top of the mat. Many bogs are surrounded by black spruce trees, which grow well in wet conditions.

Right: Bogs dot the subarctic landscape.

DRUNKEN FORESTS

Near the boundary of the tundra and the taiga, trees sometimes grow crooked. That's because they stand on a layer of permafrost. As the icy soil thaws in summer and freezes again in winter, the ground falls and rises. The tree roots shift up and down. The trees cannot grow straight, and they look like a drunken person walking. These forests of crooked trees are called "drunken forests."

SUBARCTIC ANIMALS

The Canadian subartic is home to a variety of animals. Moose, caribou, and bears are the largest land animals. Smaller land animals include snowshoe hares, porcupines, beavers, muskrats, and lynx. The rivers and lakes of subarctic Canada are home to whitefish, salmon, and pike. Ducks and geese also live near the water. All of these animals are very important to the Cree. Their ancestors relied on them for food, skins, and furs. Many Cree still depend on hunting and fishing.

Below: Caribou are sometimes attacked by wolverines, wolves, and bears.

Caribou

Caribou live in an area where the tundra meets the taiga. This area is known as the subarctic transition zone. Caribou eat mostly lichen. They also eat grass and moss. Caribou herds can number from just ten to thousands of animals. The herds often migrate hundreds of miles looking for fresh supplies of food. Both males, known as bulls, and females, known as cows, grow antlers.

Beavers

Beavers are rodents that live in streams and ponds. They eat the inner bark of shrubs and trees, especially poplar and birch trees. Beavers use sticks and mud to build houses called lodges. They also use sticks and mud to dam streams. The dams create ponds where beavers build their lodges. Beavers make their homes in water because they are good swimmers. Living in water also helps beavers keep safe from predators that live on land, such as foxes.

Above: A beaver's two front teeth are very sharp. Beavers use them to cut down trees.

Moose

Moose are large animals with long skinny legs. A big moose can stand as tall as 7 feet (2.1 meters) at the shoulder and can weigh up to 1,800 pounds (816.5 kilograms). Moose eat twigs, as well as plants that grow in the water. In summer, moose feed at bogs and lakes. Male moose have big shovel-shaped antlers that can grow to be 6 feet (1.8 meters) across. Female moose do not have antlers.

A GOOD PLACE TO HIBERNATE

Many subarctic animals hibernate in winter. Examples include ground squirrels and marmots (*right*). The animals eat lots of food during summer to get fat. In fall, they crawl into protected places, such as holes in the ground or caves. They stay there all winter. Hibernating is not the same as sleeping, but it is similar. The animal's breathing and heart rate slow down. The animal hardly moves. It survives on the stored fat in its body. It doesn't have to use energy looking for food outside in the cold. When the weather warms up in spring, the animal slowly starts moving again. Its breathing and heart rate return to normal. Then the animal goes outside to find food for another season.

EARLY CREE HISTORY

The Cree have lived in Canada for thousands of years. Their ancestors probably came to North America between 10,000 and 25,000 years ago. During this period, a land bridge linked northern Asia and Alaska. This bridge has since been covered by the sea. Many scientists think prehistoric Asian hunters crossed the bridge into Alaska, probably following animal herds. Over thousands of years, the hunters moved south and east, down through North America and into Central and South America. The Cree's ancestors spread eastward across Canada.

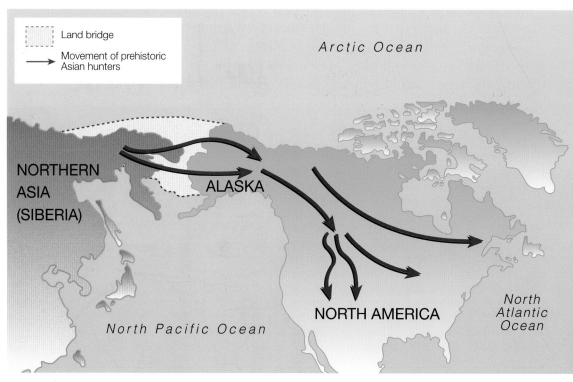

Land bridge

Movement of prehistoric Asian hunters

Arctic Ocean

NORTHERN ASIA (SIBERIA)

ALASKA

NORTH AMERICA

North Pacific Ocean

North Atlantic Ocean

Living Off the Land

The early Cree ate mostly caribou and fish, as well as beavers, bears, hares, ducks, and geese. They hunted with bows and arrows and spears. They traveled across rivers and lakes by canoe in summer. In winter, they used toboggans and snowshoes to travel over ice and snow. The Cree traveled and lived in small family groups. In winter, when food was scarce, only a few families traveled together. In summer, when it was easy to find food for many people, as many as twenty families lived and traveled together.

Above: In the past, Cree used toboggans and showshoes to travel across ice and snow. Some modern Cree continue this practice.

Below: Ancient Cree hunted American black bears for food. Modern Cree are allowed to hunt only small numbers of black bears for their furs. American black bears can eat as much as 44 pounds (20 kilograms) of food a day!

Friends and Enemies

The Cree often traded with other First Nations groups that lived below the tree line. Neighboring peoples exchanged pottery, copper, stone, and other goods. The Cree did not trade with the people who lived north of the tree line, however. These were the Inuit people, or Eskimos. They were enemies of groups to the south.

MAKING STONE TOOLS—WATCH YOUR EYES!

The early Cree and other First Nations groups made tools from stone. Examples include arrowheads and knives with razor-sharp edges. Craftsmen made these tools by hitting a piece of antler against flint or another hard rock. They chipped away the rock's edges to shape the tool. There were no safety glasses in those days, and toolmakers had to be careful. A stone splinter in the eye was painful and could blind a craftsperson.

THE CONTACT PERIOD

I n the 1600s, French and English fur traders came to Canada. They set up trading posts, and Indian trappers brought beaver furs to the posts. The European traders made money by selling these furs back in Europe. The furs were made into felt hats, which were fashionable at the time. In exchange for furs, the Europeans gave the Indians metal tools, weapons, food, cloth, and other goods. Gradually, the Cree and other native people came to depend on these goods. Because fur trapping took so much time, Cree had less time to hunt. Their traditional ways began to change.

Above: Millions of beaver skins were exported from North America to Europe from the 1600s through to the 1800s.

Left: Furs at a trading post in Alberta, Canada. The fur trade changed the lifestyle of the Cree. Instead of traveling across the land hunting for food, the Cree began to settle near European trading posts. They traded fur for food and other supplies.

Fighting for Territory

In 1670, a large English firm, the Hudson's Bay Company, set up trading posts in the Hudson Bay region of Canada. The Cree were one of the first native groups to trade with the company. The English gave the Cree guns in exchange for furs. Other Indians, including the Dakota and Iroquois, also traded with the Europeans. The Indians soon began to war among themselves over fur-trapping territory. The Cree fought with guns and were able to defeat the neighboring groups, who used only bows and arrows.

Above: Hudson's Bay Company workers prepare to set off on an expedition to find new trade routes.

Trading and Trapping

The Cree were eager to trade with Europeans. Trade goods made their lives easier, but they had to trap a lot to get these goods. Near the trading posts, some Cree became dependent on traders for food when animals near the posts were all killed. Others endured hungry years when trapping took time away from hunting.

More Europeans

European missionaries arrived in Cree country with the fur traders. The missionaries were Christian teachers. They wanted the Cree to accept the Christian God. They told the Cree their old beliefs were evil. The first missionaries were Roman Catholics from France. Protestant missionaries came with the English traders. Gradually, the missionaries convinced many Cree to become Christians.

OUTSIDE DISEASES

Some Europeans who came to North America were sick with smallpox and other diseases. The diseases spread to the Cree and other Native Americans. The native people had no natural resistance to these diseases. Cree healers using traditional remedies could not cure the sick. Many native people died. Smallpox hit the Attikamek Cree in the mid-1600s, nearly wiping out the whole group. Smallpox struck the Cree again in 1784 and 1838.

A NEW WAY OF LIFE

During the 1700s and 1800s, more and more Europeans came to Canada. They built farms, roads, and cities. Most cities were south of Cree territory, but some Europeans came to northern areas. They competed with the native people for game, and the Cree sometimes went hungry. Some Cree were forced onto reserves (known as reservations in the United States). Others moved closer to trading posts, where they knew they wouldn't starve.

Left: This illustration depicts a European trapper in the early 1900s setting a beaver trap in a stream.

Difficult Times

In the 1900s, life grew more difficult for the Cree and other First Nations groups. Some Cree still hunted and fished. Others still worked as fur trappers. But as Canada became more modern, it became harder for the Cree to make a living from the land. Some Cree left the countryside to find work in towns and cities. But many Cree had no education and few job skills. They could not earn much money.

Help from the Government

Finally, in the mid-1900s, the Canadian government began to help the Cree and other First Nations people. The government set up welfare programs, housing facilities, nursing stations, and schools in native communities. The Cree began to adopt modern ways.

Left: As North America became more developed, the Cree found it difficult to continue their old way of life.

Sent Away to School

In the late 1940s, the Canadian government began to send Cree and other Native American children to residential, or boarding, schools. These schools were run by different Christian churches. At the schools, students were allowed to speak only English or French. Teachers told students their native traditions were backward and inferior to Christian traditions. Many Cree students returned home ashamed of who they were. They had some education, but they hadn't learned about their ancient traditions. After years of being away at school, some Cree youth could no longer speak their own language. They could not even talk to their own parents and grandparents.

FROM BUFFALO TO OXEN TO TRACTORS

The Plains Cree live in the Canadian provinces of Saskatchewan and Alberta. They once hunted buffalo (*below*) for their meat and hides. By the end of the 1800s, almost all the buffalo on the plains had been killed by white hunters. The Plains Cree had to find new ways to make a living. They learned about farming. With very little equipment, they began to grow wheat and other crops. They started pulling plows by hand but soon trained oxen to do the heavy work. Some modern Plains Cree operate huge farms with heavy machinery.

THE IMPACT OF PROGRESS

In the late 1900s, outsiders began to come to Cree lands. They wanted to make changes. For example, the Canadian government wanted to build dams across rivers in Cree territory. Other groups wanted to log on Cree lands and dig for valuable minerals. Some outsiders wanted to hunt animals in Cree territory. The Cree weren't happy about the changes. They wanted to protect their land and animals. They didn't want outsiders deciding how their land would be used.

Below: The La Grande complex is a number of hydroelectric dams and plants built across the La Grande River in Quebec, Canada. The dams flooded land where the Cree once fished and hunted. This aerial picture shows a section of one of the dams.

Above: The main operations center of the La Grande 2-A dam

La Grande Complex

Starting in the late 1970s, the Quebec government began building a series of dams across the La Grande River near James Bay. Many people in Quebec were happy about the dams, which were built to supply electricity to cities. But the James Bay Cree, who lived near the dams, were angry. To build the dams, the government flooded a big Cree hunting and fishing area. The soil in this area contained poisonous mercury, which dissolved into the water. Fish absorbed the mercury, and many Cree fell ill when they ate contaminated fish.

Fighting Back

The Cree protested about the dams. The Canadian government and Hydro-Quebec, the government-owned company that built the dams, finally agreed to pay millions of dollars to the Cree to make up for the damage to their lands. It also set up job training, educational, and financial programs to help people who had been hurt by the dams, such as hunters and fishermen. Finally, the agreement gave the Cree more say in how their lands would be used in the future.

HYDROELECTRICITY: CLEAN POWER?

The La Grande River dams use the force of rushing water to create hydroelectricity. Hydroelectricity is often called "clean" power because it doesn't cause air pollution. But hydro-electric power has several drawbacks. Hydroelectric plants are usually created by damming rivers. The dams flood large areas of land, destroying the animals and plants that live there. Building a dam is also a big project. Roads must be built to transport workers and machinery. All this construction can cause pollution and damage wildlife.

FROM HUNTERS TO FUR TRAPPERS

Before Europeans arrived in Canada, the Cree were almost completely self-sufficient. They hunted and ate the animals that lived near them. Some Cree also caught fish. The James Bay Cree sometimes hunted seals and whales. The Cree sometimes traded with neighboring groups for items that were not available in the local area, such as corn, and stones for making tools.

Men's and Women's Work

Cree men and women had specific jobs. Men hunted game and trapped animals. They did the heaviest work of moving supplies and setting up camp. They built toboggans and snowshoes. Women's main jobs were taking care of the camp, minding children, cooking, and making clothing from furs and skins. Everyone needed warm clothes for winter. Making all this clothing was an important job.

Left: This Cree woman is preparing fish to be smoked over a fire. Smoking the fish helps preserve it.

Hunting Game

The Cree used spears and traps to hunt large animals such as caribou. They used several different methods. Sometimes, they speared caribou from boats as the animals swam across rivers. On land, hunters sometimes yelled and scared the caribou into funnel-shaped traps made out of brush and wood. Other hunters would be waiting to spear the animals when they entered the traps.

Left: A Cree hunter carries his catch of geese. Many Cree men still hunt to feed their families.

Right: A Cree woman picks cranberries. These berries were sometimes used to make a preserved meat dish known as pemmican.

The Transition

The European fur trade turned the Cree economy upside down. In exchange for furs, the Europeans gave the Cree guns, cloth, and metal knives and pots. In many ways, trading fur for cloth and tools was a good deal for the Cree. Trapping beavers took less time than making fur clothing and stone tools. Cooking in an iron pot was much easier than traditional Cree cooking, which involved boiling water with heated rocks.

Cloth, guns, and metal tools made life easier for the Cree. They quickly adapted to the new goods and technology. But they also came to depend on fur trading for their livelihood. Gradually, the Cree mixed the old and new ways of life, but living off the land got harder and harder.

THE TRAPPER'S TOOLS

The first Cree fur trappers made traps out of natural materials. Deadfall traps were made of pieces of wood, set up to fall and kill animals. Snares, traps designed to entangle animals, were made of animal sinew or braided plant fiber. Later, trappers used metal snares and traps, including steel traps with spring-powered jaws. These traps snapped shut when an animal stepped on them, trapping the animal's leg.

MORE ECONOMIC CHANGES

The Canadian fur business thrived for several hundred years. At first, Cree trappers traded furs for European-made goods. Later, they exchanged furs for money. The furs were shipped to Europe and other places, where they were made into hats, coats, and other items of clothing. But, gradually, fashions changed. By the early 1800s, fur hats had become less popular in Europe. In addition, trappers killed animals in great numbers. The animals began to grow scarce. With fewer animals and fewer people buying furs, the fur business slowed down.

Below: Cree use caribou fur to make clothing such as mittens, coats, and moccasins.

The Anti-Fur Movement

In the mid-1900s, some people began to speak out against the fur business. Animal rights groups argued that steel-jawed leg traps were cruel and caused animals great pain. In the late 1900s, the European Economic Community, an alliance of European governments, banned the import of fur into Europe. Fur prices crashed, and the Cree lost an important source of income.

Finding New Jobs

Despite the fur ban in Europe, some Cree still work in the fur business. They sell furs to China, the United States, and other countries. Other Cree work for the Canadian government or for Cree organizations. Construction, mining, and logging companies also provide jobs for some Cree people.

But these jobs are usually far from home. They often last for only a few months. Big cities offer more jobs than rural areas. Many Cree people have left their remote communities to find jobs in big Canadian cities such as Quebec and Ontario.

Left: Some Cree have found jobs in the construction industry. They use modern methods to build houses in urban areas as well as in their own communities.

THE FUR INDUSTRY

Because of animal rights protests, the fur business has changed its practices. New traps are lined with rubber, which causes less pain. Many fur-bearing animals are now raised from birth on ranches. But some fur-bearing animals are still trapped in the wild. After the animals are skinned, fur trappers stretch the animal skins onto frames (*right*) to dry.

TEPEES AND LODGES

The Cree built several different kinds of houses depending on where they lived. Some Cree lived in tepees, which were cone-shaped tents made from animal skins. Other Cree lived in wooden dwellings. These homes did not provide much protection from cold weather. People needed to wear warm clothes and build fires inside the houses to stay warm in winter. A hole in the middle of the roof allowed smoke to escape from the house.

Below: A Cree couple assembles the frame of a traditional winter tent.

Natural Building Materials

The Cree used natural materials to make their homes. They usually made a frame out of light wooden poles. They covered the frame with animal hides, tree branches, strips of bark, mats of woven rushes, or pieces of sod. Some homes had room for one family. Other homes were big enough for several families.

On the Move

Cree homes were temporary. When the Cree could not find animals to hunt, they moved to a new spot and built new houses. They used snowshoes to walk on snowy ground. They traveled in birch-bark canoes on rivers and on toboggans over ice and hard snow. When traveling on foot, people often used a sling called a tumpline to drag

Above: This Cree woman earns money preparing hides in her home. The floor is covered with tree branches to help keep the house warm.

their belongings behind them. In summer, the Cree often camped near lakes, which were good fishing spots. In winter, people built their homes wherever they could find the most food.

Settling Down

With the start of the fur trade, the Cree began to settle near European trading posts. Instead of tents and lodges, Cree people built log cabins near the trading posts. Later, many Cree moved into modern-style houses built by the Canadian government.

SNOWSHOES

Cree people wore snowshoes (*right*) to travel across deep snow. The snowshoes came in many shapes and sizes. One type was 7 feet (2.1 meters) long and narrow, with pointed ends. This shoe was good for walking on soft snow. Other snowshoes were more rounded. Snowshoes were made of wooden frames and woven leather webs. The leather was sometimes decorated with bits of red yarn or cloth. Modern snowshoes are usually made from aluminum or plastic.

MODERN CREE COMMUNITIES

About 30 percent of modern Cree people live in big cities. The rest live on reserves or in rural communities. In the United States, some Cree live at the Rocky Boy's Indian Reservation in Montana. Even Cree who live far from big cities have very modern lives. They use telephones, cars, and computers, just like other Canadians. Their towns look just like many other towns in Canada and the United States.

Below: An aerial view of the Cree community of Mistassini in Quebec, Canada

Above: Many Cree towns can be reached by road, but some towns can be reached only by airplanes.

Growth in Cree Territory

In the past, some Cree communities could be reached only by boat or airplane, because there were no roads there. In recent years, many Cree lands have become more connected to the rest of Canada. Mining, logging, and other companies have set up businesses in Cree territory. New roads and facilities have been built along with the new businesses. Many tourists also visit the north to hunt, fish, and explore wilderness areas.

Positive and Negative

The new building projects and businesses are both good and bad. Mining, logging, and construction companies provide jobs for Cree workers. Roads help the Cree because it's cheaper to bring in food and supplies by truck than by boat or airplane. On the other hand, dam building, mining, and other kinds of industry can damage the land, kill animals, and cause pollution. The Cree want to protect their ancient hunting and fishing grounds. They don't want outsiders deciding how their homelands will be used.

FIRST NATIONS IN THE CITY

In big Canadian cities (*below*), Cree people can meet other First Nations people from many backgrounds. They can support each other in their work and activities, such as attending college. They can also choose from a wide range of careers. Cree who live in rural areas don't have the same kinds of job and educational opportunities as urban Cree.

MAKING IT FROM SCRATCH

At first, everything the Cree needed—food, clothing, and building materials—came from the land around them. They made clothes from animal hides and furs. They built their homes from wood and other natural materials. But living off the land was not easy. Winters were very cold, and food was often scarce.

Below: Cree people have lived off the land for centuries. These Cree fishers are breaking holes in the ice so they can set a fishing net under the ice.

Animals for Clothing

In the cold subarctic winter, warm clothes could make the difference between life and death. Fur was the warmest material available. People wore fur jackets and parkas in winter, along with moccasins and leggings made from animal hide.

Above: This Cree woman is softening moose hide.

Moccasins were stuffed with grass or worn with rabbit-fur socks for extra warmth. People slept on bear, caribou, and moose furs. Women treated animal skins with a mixture of the animal's brains, liver, and fat. This mixture softened the skins so they could be made into clothing.

Left and below: These mittens and slippers are made from deer hide.

Animals for Food

The Cree mostly ate meat and fish. They hunted large animals such as caribou, moose, and deer and smaller animals like snowshoe hares and porcupines. They caught whitefish, salmon, pike, and pickerel in lakes and rivers. Hunters shot ducks and geese in spring and fall. Women dried and smoked some of the meat and fish, preserving it for winter, when food was hard to find. In summer the Cree picked berries. When European traders arrived, they brought new foods to the Cree, such as flour and tea.

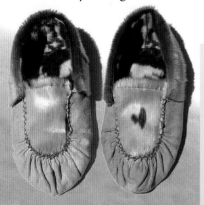

PEMMICAN

Pemmican was a popular Cree food. It was made from dried bits of caribou, moose, or buffalo meat, mixed with fat and sometimes berries. It was a favorite with fur trappers because it was easy to carry on long journeys. Trappers ate pemmican plain, or boiled with flour or peas to make a hearty stew. Sometimes trappers traded extra pemmican for other goods.

BALANCING OLD AND NEW

Modern Cree people buy most of their food in stores. They wear modern store-bought clothing. Although the Cree no longer live off the land like their ancestors, they still carry on some of their ancient traditions. For example, many Cree still practice traditional crafts and enjoy eating wild game.

Below: Introduced by traders, bannock is a simple bread that is delicious but not very nutritious.

Country Food and Store Food

Many modern Cree still hunt, fish, and collect berries for food. They call this food country food because it comes from the countryside. Country food is fresh and nutritious. More importantly, it represents the close relationship the Cree have with the land. The Cree prefer country food to store-bought food, called store food. Store food doesn't hold any special meaning for the Cree. It's usually more expensive and less nutritious than country food. For example, country food such as caribou and seal meat usually has more protein, vitamins, and calcium than meat sold in stores.

Above: Most store food is not as healthy to eat as country food. Store food also has little cultural meaning for the Cree.

Back to the Land

The modern Cree want to preserve their connection with the land. Cree leaders want to teach Cree youth about their cultural heritage. Many Cree bands organize culture camps for students. At these camps, Cree elders teach young people traditional skills such as working with hides, catching fish, and doing beadwork. Sometimes participants visit a sweat lodge or learn to paddle an old-style canoe. Culture camps are often held in remote areas. They give young people a chance to live the type of life their ancestors did.

HOLDING ON TO HISTORY

For thousands of years, Cree elders told stories about their culture. But after the Europeans arrived, it became harder to pass on the old tales. Many Cree died because of diseases brought by the Europeans. There were fewer elders left to tell stories. Later, many Cree children were sent to residential schools. They no longer learned stories from their elders. Finally, modern devices like televisions took the place of storytelling in Cree communities. In Canada, a few radio and television networks broadcast programs in Cree and other native languages. Cree leaders hope that these programs will help native people preserve their tales and traditions.

CREE ARTS AND CRAFTS

Traditionally, Cree women made beautiful and fancy beadwork on clothing. Some everyday Cree objects, such as baskets, were also beautiful pieces of art. Modern Cree artists still make beautiful crafts using materials such as animal skins, furs, birch bark, and wood. They also make beaded craft items. Modern Cree artists practice some crafts that their ancestors did not, such as painting and etching. Many Cree communities have shops that sell the work of local craftspeople.

Right: This Cree craftsman is making an ornament from tamarack twigs. A tamarack is a type of pine tree found in North America and Europe.

Fancy Beadwork

Before the Europeans arrived, Cree women decorated clothing and other objects with beads made from porcupine quills, shells, rocks, and clay. In Quebec, Cree people wore beaded hoods, which were so long that they almost touched the ground. European traders brought new

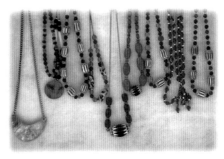

Above: The Cree traded furs for beads brought by the Europeans.

kinds of beads in a wide range of sizes, colors, and materials. Cree women liked the new beads, especially the small colorful glass ones. They used these beads to embroider flowers and fancy patterns onto clothing and moccasins. Some of the patterns might have been based on English designs, which Cree women saw at Hudson's Bay Company trading posts.

Birch Bark Containers

The Cree made baskets and boxes from birch bark and decorated them with pictures of ducks and other animals and with geometric designs. Designs were made in two different ways. One method involved painting on bark with vegetable dyes. Another technique involved tracing a pattern onto dark bark. The inside of the pattern was then scraped away, exposing lighter bark beneath. Once the Cree got metal pots from European traders, they made fewer birch bark containers.

Left: Renowned Cree artist Tim Whiskeychan of Waskaganish, Quebec, proudly displays a painting done on animal hide.

REACHING AFAR

Modern Cree writers, actors, and artists are making an impression far outside of Cree communities. George Littlechild, for instance, has written many books for children. Tina Keeper, Gordon Tootoosis, and Tantoo Cardinal are Cree-Métis actors who have appeared in television shows and movies. Painter Allen Sapp and mixed-media artist Jane Ash Poitras are just two of many well-known Cree artists whose works are shown all over North America.

THE CREE LANGUAGE

The Cree language is similar to other languages spoken by Indians in northeastern North America. These languages are called Algonquian. There are ten dialects, or regional variations, of the Cree language. Some dialects are very different, so Cree people from different places don't always understand each other. One dialect, called Mitchif, or French Cree, includes many French words. The Cree language is one of the most widely spoken native languages in North America.

ᐧᐊᑳᑭᐱᑕᐦᒃ ᑎᑕᐱᐱᐟᐤ

Waskaganish Local Annual General Assembly '96
"Creating a Healthier Cree Nation for a Brighter Future"

ᐁᑯᓐᐧᐊᕆᐳᐁᑯᑕᕂᑕᐤ ᐃᐱᐱᒥ ᐧ
ᐃᑕᕂᑭᕆᐳᑕᐤ ᐊᓴᐅ ᐃᔕ ᓇᕂᒐᕂᒣᐅ

Above: This sign features English words as well as Cree symbols.

Below: Several hundred Cree children attend the Ecole Wiinibekuu School in Waskaganish, Quebec.

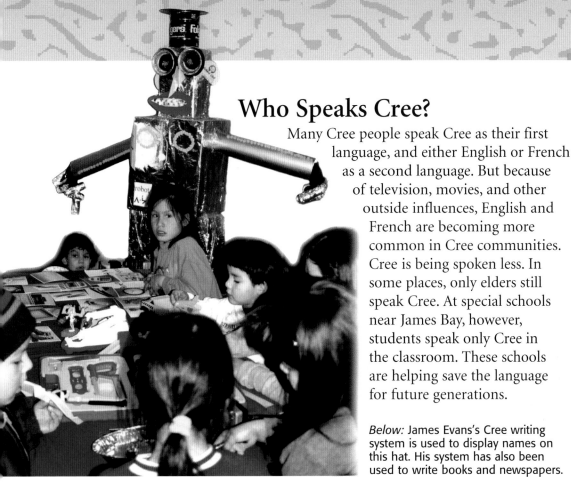

Who Speaks Cree?

Many Cree people speak Cree as their first language, and either English or French as a second language. But because of television, movies, and other outside influences, English and French are becoming more common in Cree communities. Cree is being spoken less. In some places, only elders still speak Cree. At special schools near James Bay, however, students speak only Cree in the classroom. These schools are helping save the language for future generations.

Below: James Evans's Cree writing system is used to display names on this hat. His system has also been used to write books and newspapers.

Above: Cree elementary students display their creations at a regional science fair.

A Written Cree Language

Before the Europeans came to North America, the Cree did not have a writing system. They passed down legends and tales by word of mouth. In the 1830s, missionary James Evans wrote down the Cree language using symbols. In areas where many people speak Cree, Evans's system is still used. Where only a few people speak Cree, most people write the language using the English or French alphabet.

DIFFERENT DIALECTS

Because different Cree groups lived far from each other for long periods, they developed different grammar, vocabulary, and pronunciation. For example, the Cree words for "I" and "you" are *ni'ya* and *ki'ya* in most of Alberta and Saskatchewan. But in most of Manitoba and Ontario, *ni'na* and *ki'na* mean "I" and "you."

THE SPIRIT WORLD

Cree people lived close to nature for thousands of years. They believed that spirits inhabited animals, plants, and everything else in the natural world. It was important to the Cree to have good relationships with animal spirits, since they relied on animals for food. When Christian missionaries arrived with the fur traders, many Cree people became Catholics or Protestants. Often, they continued to practice their old religion together with Christianity.

Left: These bear skulls have been placed high up in a tree so that other animals can't disturb them. The Cree consider this practice a sign of respect to the spirits of animals they have killed.

Honoring the Spirits

Cree hunters treated animals with respect. Without animals, there would be no food. If people insulted an animal, the Cree believed, that animal would not allow itself to be caught or killed. Bears and beavers were especially respected because they were important sources of food and furs.

The Power of Shamans

Shamans were men and women who had special powers for communicating with animal spirits. They used their powers to tell hunters where to find game. Some shamans looked into the future by burning the shoulder bones of caribou or hares. The cracks and breaks in the burned bones told the shamans about future events or where to find good hunting areas.

Manitou and Windigo

Most Cree bands believed in a supreme spirit known as Manitou. Historians aren't sure how this belief started. They think white missionaries may have introduced the idea of a supreme spirit when they were trying to explain their Christian God to the Cree. The Cree saw Manitou as a helping spirit, who protected those who honored him from evil and sorcery. The Cree also believed in an evil human-eating monster called Windigo.

Left: Shamans sometimes used the shoulder bones of caribou to predict the future. Caribou fur was also made into clothes and used to cover Cree tents.

TOADMAN—THE FROG SPIRIT

Toadman was the frog spirit. He lived under the mud. He was handsome, but his skin was very pale, like the belly of a frog. Cree legend says that Toadman saw a woman picking berries near a marsh one day. She started sinking in the mud, and Toadman caught her. She tried to escape but could not break free. Toadman took her to his home under the mud, and she became his wife.

CREE RITUALS

The Cree practiced many rituals that helped them pray and communicate with the spirit world. In the 1900s, some of these rituals began to die out. White school and church leaders frowned on the old beliefs, which they called backward. In addition, Cree people hunted less and less during the 1900s. So ancient beliefs about animal spirits grew less important. In recent years, though, the Cree have started to revive some of their old religious practices.

Below: Christian missionaries disapproved of ancient Cree rituals. Some Cree attend this church near James Bay, Canada.

Cree Funerals

When a Cree person died, his or her relatives washed the body. They wrapped it in birch or spruce bark for burial. If the person died in winter, when the earth was frozen, the body was placed on the ground in its bark coffin. Hunting weapons, clothing, and animal bones were placed on the grave or hung nearby.

Left: A modern Cree grave at a burial site in Canada

The Shaking Tent

The shaking tent ritual helped the Cree communicate with animal spirits. First, people built a small cone-shaped tent, about 4 feet (1.2 meters) wide with an opening at the top. It was covered with hides, bark, or reeds. Around dusk, a shaman, called the shaking tent master, went into the tent. He sang songs and beat on a drum to call the animal spirits. People outside could tell that the spirits had come when the tent started to shake. They could hear the spirits make noises. Sometimes, people saw strange lights come from the tent. From inside the tent, the shaking tent master could talk with people and spirits far away, find lost objects, and battle evil forces.

TENT POLES

The Muskeg Lake Cree of Saskatchewan made their homes in tents. Each tent pole (*below*) stood for a virtue. These virtues were obedience, respect, humility, happiness, faith, kinship, cleanliness, thankfulness, sharing, love, strength, good child rearing, hope, protection, and control.

Sweat Lodges

The Cree used sweat lodges to purify their bodies and souls. Sweat lodges were small round huts, heated by hot rocks. People inside poured water on the rocks to make steam. The steam and heat made the people sweat. The Cree believed that sweating helped clean the body and mind.

GATHERING TOGETHER

In earlier centuries, the Cree found lots of ways to celebrate and have a good time. In the evenings, people danced and sang songs. They listened to elders tell stories, which often taught important lessons. Stories and songs also helped pass the time on long, cold winter nights. When the Cree became fur traders, they gathered together at trading posts for feasts, dancing, and gambling. In modern times, the Cree still like to get together and celebrate. Many Cree people observe Christian holidays, such as Christmas and Easter. They observe Canadian holidays, too. Finally, the Cree often get together with other First Nations groups to honor their Native American culture.

Below: Cree children play with a parachute during Spring Festival celebrations. The Cree celebrate the Spring Festival to welcome the arrival of spring.

National Aboriginal Day

In 1996, June 21 was proclaimed National Aboriginal Day in Canada. *Aboriginal* is another name for native people from around the world. On this day, the Cree and other First Nations people hold a big celebration. All over Canada, they hold parades, give feasts, have dances, and display native arts.

Powwows

The Cree also get together with other First Nations groups at powwows. Powwows are festivals at which Indians of many backgrounds gather to celebrate their culture together. The festivals always include dance contests. Contestants dress in their best native clothes and dance to drumbeats and singing. At the end of the powwow, everyone joins in on the last dance.

Left: Cree children at a powwow. Powwow celebrations usually last for four days.

WORKING TOGETHER

In earlier centuries, Cree people needed to share and help one another. Without cooperation, they could not survive in the tough environment. They feared the spirits would punish them if they misbehaved. Family groups often chose a leader, usually a good hunter who was smart and generous. But the leader did not rule the other people in the group. Instead, everyone made decisions together. Family and the wider community continue to be important to the Cree (*right*).

FUN AND GAMES

The early Cree liked sports and games. Some games helped men and boys practice their hunting skills. Games of chance taught people about life in a harsh environment. They realized that sometimes survival was out of their control.

Traditional Games

Some Cree played lacrosse, a Native American game played with sticks and a ball. Running and playing hard made boys strong for hunting. The Cree also played tug-of-war and made string puzzles. Boys learned to become hunters by playing with toy bows and arrows and peashooters. In a game called snow goose, one boy would swing a wooden or stone target around in the air. Other boys would sit or kneel and try to hit or catch the target. All children played hide-and-seek. Cree girls played with carved wooden dolls.

Left: A lacrosse stick is called a crosse. It is made from aluminum, wood, or graphite. The strings can be made from rawhide, gut, string, or linen cord.

Modern Games

Modern Cree play modern sports such as softball. Ice hockey is especially popular. Many Cree first learned to play hockey when they went to residential schools in the 1940s. They started their own teams when they returned home. In modern times, Cree community teams regularly compete against each other. Several Cree hockey players, including Johnathan Cheechoo, play in the National Hockey League.

Regional Contests

The Saskatchewan Indian Summer and Winter Games are like a mini-Olympics for First Nations children. The winter games are held around Easter. Winter events include hockey and volleyball. The summer games are held in late July and early August. Events include softball and soccer.

Left: These Cree boys are about to start a snowshoe race during Spring Festival celebrations.

NORTH AMERICAN INDIGENOUS GAMES

The North American Indigenous Games have been held every two years since 1990. Native athletes from all over the United States and Canada compete in many sports. Events include modern sports such as basketball and traditional games from many Native American cultures. The 2002 games will be held in Winnipeg, Manitoba. More than eight thousand First Nations, Métis, and Inuit athletes, coaches, and officials will take part. Three thousand musicians, dancers, and other performers, as well as five thousand volunteers, will contribute to the massive gathering.

GLOSSARY

Arctic: the northernmost region on Earth, containing the North Pole, the Arctic Ocean, and surrounding lands

Arctic Circle: an imaginary line around the northern part of the Earth. The line is 1,624 miles (2,613 kilometers) south of the North Pole.

dialect: a regional variation of a language, with slight differences in pronunciation, grammar, and vocabulary

global warming: the gradual rising of temperatures on Earth, possibly caused by air pollution

hibernate: to pass the winter in a resting state, similar to sleep

hydroelectricity: electric power created by rushing water

indigenous people: the people who originally lived in a country when it came into contact with outsiders

land bridge: a narrow strip of land that connects two land masses

migrate: to travel to a new place, often in search of food or other resources

missionaries: people who try to convert others to their religion

nomadic: moving from place to place, without a settled home

permafrost: the frozen soil of Arctic and subarctic lands

predators: animals that survive by killing and eating other animals

regional: belonging to or typical of a particular geographic area

reserves: lands in Canada set aside for First Nations use. In the United States, reserves are called reservations.

shaman: a person who can communicate with the spirit world, tell the future, and use magic to heal the sick

subarctic: the region on earth just south of the Arctic Circle

taiga: the evergreen forests of subarctic regions

tumpline: a sling connected to a strap slung across the forehead, used for hauling loads

tundra: the treeless plains of Arctic regions

FINDING OUT MORE

Books

Bartok, Mira, and Christine Ronan. *Indians of the Great Plains.* Glenview IL: Good Year Books, 1994.

Dorion, Betty F. *Melanie Bluelake's Dream.* Regina, Canada: Coteau Books, 1998.

Linderman, Frank Bird. *Indian Why Stories.* Mineola, NY: Dover Publications, 1995.

Norman, Howard A. *Trickster and the Fainting Birds.* San Diego, CA: Harcourt Brace, 1999.

Terry, Michael Bad Hand. *Daily Life in a Plains Indian Village, 1868.* New York; Houghton Mifflin, 1999.

Videos

Cree Hunters of Mistassini. National Film Board of Canada, 1974.

Flooding Job's Garden. Distributed by First Run/Icarus, 1991.

Power: The James Bay Cree vs. Hydro-Quebec. Distributed by Cineflix Inc., 1996.

Websites

<http://www.creeculture.ca/e/institute/index.html>

<http://www.mandow.ca/share.htm>

<http://www.nisto.com/cree/syllabic/>

<http://www.schoolnet.ca/aboriginal/Plains_Cree/index-e.html>

<http://www.sicc.sk.ca/>

Organizations

Assembly of First Nations
1 Nicholas Street, Suite 1002
Ottawa, Ontario K1N 7B7
Tel: (613) 241-6789
Website: <http://www.afn.ca/>

Cree-Naskapi Commission
222 Queen Street, Suite 305
Ottawa, Ontario, K1P 5V9
Tel: (888) 236-6603 or (613) 234-4288
Website: <http://www.atreide.net/cnc>

Embassy of the Cree Nation
24 Bayswater Avenue
Ottawa, Ontario, K1Y 2E4
Tel: (613) 761-1655

INDEX

ABOUT THE AUTHOR

Deborah Robinson lives in Lyme, New Hampshire, with her partner, Jay. Deborah is a research fellow at Dartmouth College's Institute of Arctic Studies. She works on a variety of projects including the environment, rights of native peoples, caribou, and fish. She also teaches geography, environmental studies, and anthropology at the Community College of Vermont. She holds a bachelor's degree in writing and literature from the University of Michigan and a master's degree in geography from McGill University.

PICTURE CREDITS